SMALL

SKEWERS, SLIDERS, AND OTHER PARTY EATS

BITES

SMALL

SKEWERS, SLIDERS, AND OTHER PARTY EATS

BITES

ELIZA CROSS

GIBBS SMITH
TO ENRICH AND INSPIRE HUMANKIND

To Corine van Bodegom,
who adds sparkle to every party.

First Edition
21 20 19 18   5 4

Text © 2017 Eliza Cross
Photographs © 2017 Jessica Nicosia-Nadler

Published by
Gibbs Smith
P.O. Box 667
Layton, Utah 84041

1.800.835.4993 orders
www.gibbs-smith.com

Designed by Katie Jennings Campbell
Printed and bound in Hong Kong

Gibbs Smith books are printed on either recycled, 100%
post-consumer waste, FSC-certified papers or on paper
produced from sustainable PEFC-certified forest/controlled
wood source. Learn more at www.pefc.org.

Library of Congress Cataloging-in-Publication Data
Names: Cross, Eliza, author. | Nicosia-Nadler, Jessica,
photographer.
Title: Small bites : skewers, sliders, and other party eats /
Eliza Cross
Photographs by Jessica Nicosia-Nadler.
Description: First edition. | Layton, Utah : Gibbs Smith,
[2017] |
Includes index.
Identifiers: LCCN 2017003908 | ISBN 9781423647850
(jacketless hardcover)
Subjects: LCSH: Appetizers. | LCGFT: Cookbooks.
Classification: LCC TX740 .C744 2017 | DDC 641.81/2--dc23
LC record available at https://lccn.loc.gov/2017003908

ISBN: 978-1-4236-4785-0

Contents

INTRODUCTION

Have you ever perused a restaurant menu and been far more tempted by the appetizer offerings than the entrées? I know I have. Perhaps it's because the starters often feature tantalizing ingredients, intriguing preparations, and manageable portion sizes. Or maybe it's because appetizers are synonymous with parties, and party food is meant to be fun.

When I entertain at home, I love to prepare hors d'oeuvres. After all, appetizers are meant to be shared with others. For me, a few platters of lovingly prepared canapés mark the joy of gathering with friends and family over good food and drink.

I especially love small appetizers that combine creativity and great flavor in just a bite or two. The best hors d'oeuvres are pleasing to both the palate and the eye, conveying to your guests that you made a special effort to create a festive start to your gathering. The recipes in this collection each have elements that can be prepared in advance, so you can enjoy your own party instead of being stuck in the kitchen doing prep work.

The book is divided into four sections. A selection of basic recipes will guide you in preparing miniature rolls, crisps, and crostini, so you can build your own tasty creations from the bottom up. Finger foods are small, unfussy bites that can be eaten out of hand—like tiny artichoke-sausage pizzas drizzled with a balsamic glaze, or miniature Mexican tostadas served in crispy corn shells. Skewered appetizers layer a variety of flavors like sweet dried apricots stuffed with tangy chèvre and wrapped in bacon, or delicate fried artichoke hearts dipped in a lemony garlic butter. Mini sandwiches feature a variety of breads and fillings, from baby open-faced Reubens served with homemade Thousand Island dressing to a miniature version of the famous lobster roll.

When you're entertaining, I recommend choosing a pleasing selection of appetizers that vary in presentation, texture, color, temperature, and flavor. For example, you could serve a tray of hot, crispy Crab and Avocado Nachos (page 56), a platter of colorful Greek Salad on a Stick skewers (page 82), and a plate of elegant Prosciutto, Pear, Fig, and Brie Toasts (page 120). Arrange hors d'oeuvres neatly on platters, and let the food take center stage by leaving plates unadorned or choosing simple garnishes.

After trying the small bites featured in this book, you may decide to forgo the entrée at your next dinner party in favor of an assortment of tantalizing appetizers. Whether you're entertaining a small group or a large crowd, small bites offer a variety of flavors with something to please everyone. Let's start cooking and get the party started!

BASIC BITES

These easy recipes will help you create your own fresh bases, upon which you can build a countless number of appealing appetizers. Pita crisps are perfect for dipping, dunking, and holding salads and spreads. Buttery, toasted crostini can be piled high with a variety of different toppings. Tiny choux puffs made from cream puff dough are light and elegant. Bite-size mini toast cups and crispy pastry cups are both easy to make and sturdy enough to hold a variety of fillings. Miniature slider rolls are ideal for making small sandwiches. All of these bases can be prepared in advance so that the only thing left to do before the party is fill them, serve them, and accept the inevitable compliments.

Garlic Pita Crisps

Makes 36

3 pita pockets

2 tablespoons butter, melted

2 tablespoons olive oil

1 clove garlic, minced

$^1/_4$ teaspoon salt

$^1/_4$ teaspoon freshly ground black pepper

Preheat the oven to 400°F and lightly grease a baking sheet.

Cut each pita pocket in half and split the halves. Cut each half into 3 triangles; place split side up on prepared baking sheet.

In a small bowl, combine the butter, olive oil, garlic, salt, and pepper. Brush the pita triangles with the butter mixture.

Bake until golden brown, 8–12 minutes. Cool on a wire rack. Pita crisps can be stored in a tightly covered container at room temperature for up to 2 days.

Baby Sesame Slider Rolls

Makes 24

3 $\frac{1}{2}$ cups all-purpose flour

$\frac{1}{8}$ teaspoon salt

$\frac{3}{4}$ cup water

1 tablespoon rapid rise yeast

$\frac{1}{4}$ cup sugar

1 egg, lightly beaten

4 tablespoons melted butter, divided

Sesame seeds, for sprinkling

In the bowl of a stand mixer, combine the flour, salt, water, yeast, sugar, egg, and 2 tablespoons of the butter; mix for 1 minute. Using the hook attachment, continue mixing on medium-low until dough becomes smooth and elastic, 4–5 minutes. Remove bowl and cover with a clean, damp kitchen towel. Let dough rise in a warm place until doubled in size, about 1 hour.

Preheat the oven to 375°F and line 2 baking sheets with parchment paper.

Turn the dough out onto a lightly floured work surface and roll to a thickness of $\frac{1}{3}$ inch. Cut rounds using a 2-inch biscuit or cookie cutter. Gather scraps, knead briefly, re-roll, and repeat to make 24 total rounds. Arrange the rounds 2 inches apart on prepared baking sheets. Cover with a clean, damp kitchen towel and let rise until doubled in size, about 30 minutes.

Brush with the remaining 2 tablespoons butter, sprinkle with sesame seeds, and bake until golden brown, about 10–12 minutes. Cool on a wire rack to room temperature. Rolls can be stored in a tightly covered container at room temperature and are best eaten within 24 hours. Use a sharp knife to split the rolls in half just before filling.

Kobe Beef Sliders with Secret Sauce recipe on page 100.

Crispy Pastry Cups

Makes 24

¹/₂ cup cream cheese, softened

¹/₂ cup salted butter, softened

1 cup all-purpose flour

Preheat the oven to 350°F and grease two 12-cup mini muffin pans.

In a small bowl, beat the cream cheese and butter until smooth. Add flour and mix well. Shape into 24 balls. Press balls into the bottom and up the sides of prepared muffin cups.

Bake until golden brown, 10–15 minutes. Cool for 5 minutes in pan and transfer cups to a wire rack to cool completely. Cups can be stored in a tightly covered container for up to 2 days at room temperature.

Golden Crostini

Makes about 24

1 long baguette, cut into
1/2-inch-thick slices

2 tablespoons olive oil

2 tablespoons butter, melted

Set the oven to broil and arrange the rack in the middle of the oven.

In a small bowl, combine the olive oil and butter. Arrange the bread slices in a single layer on a baking sheet and brush with the butter mixture. Broil, watching carefully, until golden brown, 6–8 minutes. Crostini can be stored in a tightly covered container for up to 2 days at room temperature.

Mini Toast Cups

Makes 24 cups

Nonstick cooking spray

8 slices soft white or whole wheat bread

Preheat the oven to 450°F and lightly spray two 12-cup mini muffin pans.

Use a rolling pin to flatten the bread. Cut 3 rounds from each slice using a 2-inch fluted cookie cutter or biscuit cutter. Press the rounds into the prepared muffin pans to form shallow cups.

Bake until lightly browned, about 6 minutes. Cool on a wire rack. Cups can be stored in a tightly covered container for up to 2 days at room temperature.

Mini BLT Cups recipe on page 27.

Tiny Choux Puffs

1/2 cup water	1/2 cup all-purpose flour	2 eggs
1/4 cup butter	1/8 teaspoon salt	

Preheat the oven to 425°F and lightly grease a baking sheet.

In a saucepan, combine the water and butter and bring to a boil over medium heat. Stir in the flour and salt and cook, stirring constantly, until batter leaves sides of pan and forms a rough ball. Remove from heat.

Beat in the eggs, 1 at a time, until mixture becomes smooth. Drop by rounded teaspoons onto prepared baking sheet. Bake for 10 minutes. Reduce oven heat to 350°F and continue baking for 20 more minutes, or until puffs are golden brown. Cool on a wire rack to room temperature.

Puffs can be stored in a tightly covered container in the refrigerator for up to 2 days. Bring to room temperature before serving, and use a sharp knife to split the puffs in half just before filling.

Tarragon Chicken Salad Puffs recipe on page 91.

FINGER FOODS

Compact and easy to eat in a bite or two, finger foods are an ideal choice for a traditional cocktail party. Lighter offerings like Mini Asian Lettuce Wraps (page 37) or crispy Parmesan-Spinach Crispies (page 55) can be served with drinks as a prelude to a meal, while more substantial hors d'oeuvres like Dry-Rubbed Riblets (page 43), Tiny Twice-Baked Potatoes (page 52), or Honey-Ginger Mini Drumsticks (page 28) are perfect for a casual appetizers-only buffet.

The general rule of thumb recommended by caterers is five to seven pieces per person for a cocktail reception, and ten to twelve pieces per person for a dinnertime hors d'oeuvres party. I always prepare an extra platter or two in case the party size expands or guests' appetites are especially ravenous. If everything doesn't get eaten, any leftover finger foods make great snacks the following day.

Turkey and Cranberry Pinwheels

Makes about 40

1 (8-ounce) package cream cheese, softened

1 tablespoon milk

2 teaspoons Dijon mustard

$1/8$ teaspoon salt

$1/8$ teaspoon freshly ground black pepper

5 (10-inch) flour tortillas, room temperature

$1/2$ cup sweetened dried cranberries, chopped

2 green onions, finely chopped

$1/2$ pound deli-sliced smoked turkey

$1/2$ pound sliced Swiss cheese

In a small bowl, combine the cream cheese, milk, mustard, salt, and pepper; stir until blended. Spread mixture over each tortilla and sprinkle with dried cranberries and green onions. Layer with sliced turkey and Swiss cheese. Roll up tightly and wrap in plastic wrap. Refrigerate for at least 2 hours and up to 24 hours. Cut in $1/2$-inch slices and arrange on a serving platter.

Artichoke and Sausage Pizzas

Makes 20

1/2 cup balsamic vinegar

2 tablespoons dark brown sugar

1 pound prepared pizza dough

1 cup prepared pizza sauce

1/2 pound bulk Italian sausage, cooked, drained, and finely crumbled

3/4 cup grated mozzarella cheese

1/2 cup finely chopped canned (drained) artichoke hearts

1/3 cup finely chopped green bell pepper

To prepare the glaze, combine the balsamic vinegar and brown sugar in a small saucepan over medium heat; stir constantly until brown sugar dissolves. When mixture just starts to bubble, reduce heat to low and simmer until reduced by half, about 20 minutes. Cool to room temperature and use at once, or refrigerate in a tightly covered glass container for up to 1 week.

Preheat the oven to 400°F and line a large baking sheet with parchment paper.

Place pizza dough on a lightly floured work surface. Press and stretch dough into a 12 x 8-inch rectangle. With a 2-inch round cutter, cut dough into 20 rounds. Arrange 1 inch apart on prepared baking sheet and press gently with fingertips to make a slight rim around the edges. Spread each with 1 scant tablespoon pizza sauce. Top with sausage, cheese, artichoke hearts, and bell pepper.

Bake until cheese melts and edges are lightly browned, 8–10 minutes. Remove from oven and transfer pizzas to a wire rack to cool for 5 minutes. Drizzle with the glaze (if refrigerated, bring to room temperature) and transfer to a serving platter.

Smoked Salmon Cucumber Rounds with Lemon Dill Cream

$^3/_4$ cup cream cheese, softened

2 tablespoons sour cream

1 tablespoon fresh lemon juice

1 tablespoon minced fresh dill

$^1/_4$ teaspoon garlic powder

$^1/_8$ teaspoon salt

1 English cucumber

5 ounces smoked salmon, refrigerated

Freshly ground black pepper, for garnish

Fresh dill sprigs, for garnish

In a bowl, combine the cream cheese, sour cream, lemon juice, dill, garlic powder, and salt; stir until well blended. Transfer to a heavy-duty ziplock bag. Mixture may be used at once or refrigerated for up to 24 hours. (If refrigerated, bring to room temperature for 1 hour before using.)

Drag the tines of a fork lengthwise down the sides of the cucumber for a decorative effect. Cut the cucumber into $^1/_3$-inch-thick slices, blot on paper towels, and arrange on a serving platter. Cut $^1/_2$ inch off one of the corners of the ziplock bag, and pipe the cream cheese mixture onto the cucumber rounds. Cut small strips of the smoked salmon and arrange on top. Garnish with pepper and dill sprigs.

Tiny Corn Cakes with Avocado Pico de Gallo

Makes about 30 to 36

1/2 cup finely chopped red onion

1 jalapeño pepper, seeded and finely chopped

2 tablespoons fresh lime juice

1/3 cup chopped fresh cilantro

1 pound ripe Roma tomatoes, seeded and finely chopped

2 small avocados, peeled and finely chopped

2 teaspoons salt, divided

1/4 teaspoon freshly ground black pepper

2 cups canned or cooked corn kernels, well drained

1 (15-ounce) can creamed corn

2 eggs

1 1/2 cups grated sharp cheddar cheese

1/2 teaspoon paprika

1 1/2 cups all-purpose flour

1 teaspoon baking powder

1/2 to 3/4 cup milk

1 tablespoon vegetable oil

Combine onion, jalapeño, and lime juice in a bowl. Stir gently and let stand for 5 minutes. Stir in the cilantro, tomatoes, avocados, 1 teaspoon of salt, and pepper; reserve. (May be prepared up to 1 hour ahead and stored at room temperature. Stir before serving.)

In a large bowl, combine corn kernels, creamed corn, eggs, cheese, paprika, and remaining 1 teaspoon salt; mix well. Sift in the flour and baking powder and mix well. Slowly stir in 1/2 cup milk, adding extra if needed to make a smooth batter.

Heat a large skillet over medium heat and brush it with the oil. When oil shimmers, use a ladle to make 3-inch pancakes. Cook until bottoms are lightly browned and bubbles appear on top; flip and continue cooking until golden brown. Transfer to paper towels to drain.

Arrange warm cakes on a platter. Place a spoon in the pico so guests can spoon it over top.

Mini BLT Cups

Makes 24

6 strips bacon, cooked and finely crumbled

3/4 cup finely chopped romaine lettuce

2 Roma tomatoes, cored, seeded, and finely chopped

2 to 3 tablespoons mayonnaise

Salt and freshly ground pepper, to taste

24 Mini Toast Cups (page 16)

In a bowl, combine the bacon, lettuce, and tomatoes. Stir in the mayonnaise. Season with salt and pepper. Refrigerate filling, covered, for up to 2 hours.

Just before serving, fill each bread cup with a heaping spoon of the BLT mixture.

Photo on page 17.

Honey-Ginger Mini Drumsticks

Makes 24

24 mini chicken drumsticks*

1 (2-inch) piece fresh ginger, peeled and minced

1/4 cup low-sodium soy sauce

2 tablespoons honey

1/2 teaspoon sesame oil

1/4 teaspoon freshly ground black pepper

2 cloves garlic, minced

Sesame seeds, for garnish

Finely chopped green onions, for garnish

Rinse the drumsticks and pat dry with paper towels. In a large bowl, whisk together the ginger, soy sauce, honey, sesame oil, pepper, and garlic. Add the mini drumsticks and stir until completely coated. Cover and refrigerate for 2–6 hours, stirring occasionally.

Preheat the oven to 375°F and line a baking sheet with aluminum foil.

Drain and discard the marinade, and arrange the drumsticks on the prepared baking sheet. Bake, turning once, until drumsticks are golden brown and cooked through (165°F on an instant-read thermometer), 20–25 minutes. Arrange drumsticks on a platter, sprinkle with sesame seeds and green onions, and serve warm.

*Mini drumsticks, also known as drumettes, are the meatier halves of chicken wings. If unavailable, 12 whole chicken wings may be substituted; split at the joint to make 24 pieces, removing and discarding wing tips if necessary.

Baby Mexican Tostadas

Makes 36

1 cup shredded cooked
chicken

1/2 cup prepared salsa

1 green onion, minced

36 tortilla chip cups, such as
Tostitos Scoops

1/2 cup grated Mexican
cheese blend

1/4 cup finely chopped
romaine lettuce

1/4 cup finely chopped
avocado

1/4 cup finely chopped
tomato

1/4 cup sour cream

In a small bowl, combine the chicken, salsa, and green onion; stir with a fork to blend.
Use at once, or refrigerate in a tightly covered container for up to 1 day. (If refrigerated,
let sit at room temperature for 1 hour before proceeding.)

Preheat the oven broiler and line a baking sheet with aluminum foil.

Arrange the tortilla chip cups on the prepared baking sheet. Divide the chicken mixture
among the cups and sprinkle with the cheese. Broil, watching carefully, until cheese is
melted, 2–3 minutes. Remove from oven and cool for 5 minutes. Top each mini tostada
with the lettuce, avocado, tomato, and a small dollop of sour cream. Transfer to a
serving platter.

Crispy Lasagna Cups

Makes 24

2 teaspoons olive oil

1/4 cup finely chopped onion

1 clove garlic, minced

2 Italian sausages, casings removed

1 cup prepared marinara sauce

1/4 teaspoon Italian herb seasoning

Pinch of red pepper flakes

Salt and freshly ground black pepper, to taste

24 wonton wrappers

3/4 cup ricotta cheese

1/4 cup Parmesan cheese

1 cup finely grated mozzarella cheese

In a skillet, heat the olive oil over medium heat. Add the onion and sauté until tender, 4–5 minutes. Add the garlic and sauté until fragrant, 1 minute more. Crumble the sausages in the skillet and continue cooking, breaking up the meat with a spatula. Cook until brown and cooked through, 4–5 minutes more. Add the marinara sauce and bring to a simmer. Stir in the Italian herb seasoning, red pepper flakes, and season with salt and pepper. Reduce heat to low and cook for 2 minutes. Remove from heat and cool for 5 minutes. (Sauce can be prepared ahead and refrigerated, tightly covered, for up to 1 day. Reheat before proceeding.)

Preheat the oven to 375°F. Spray two 12-cup mini muffin pans with nonstick cooking spray. Press 1 wonton wrapper into the bottom of each muffin cup, using fingers to create a little fluted cup.

In a small bowl, stir together the ricotta and Parmesan. Spoon 1 scant tablespoon of the sauce mixture into each wonton cup. Top with 2 teaspoons of the ricotta mixture and sprinkle with 2 teaspoons mozzarella. Bake until cheese is melted and cups are golden brown, about 12 minutes. Cool for 3–5 minutes before removing from the pan. (Mini lasagna cups may be covered with plastic wrap and refrigerated for up to 24 hours. Reheat in a 350°F oven until heated through, 6–8 minutes.) Transfer to a serving platter and serve warm.

Beef Oscar Tartlets

Makes 24

¹/₂ cup plus 2 tablespoons mayonnaise, divided

2 green onions, finely minced

2 teaspoons chopped fresh tarragon, or ¹/₂ teaspoon dried tarragon

1¹/₂ teaspoons fresh lemon juice

1 teaspoon Dijon mustard

Salt and freshly ground black pepper, to taste

1 (6-ounce) can crab meat, drained and picked over for shells

2 tablespoons grated

Parmesan cheese

1 (8-ounce) can refrigerated crescent dinner rolls

6 large slices deli roast beef

24 thin stalks fresh asparagus, steamed

24 small fresh parsley sprigs

In a small bowl, stir together ¹/₂ cup of mayonnaise, green onions, tarragon, lemon juice, and Dijon mustard. Season with salt and pepper. Reserve or refrigerate, covered, for up to 1 day. (If refrigerated, let sit at room temperature for 1 hour before using.)

Preheat the oven to 350°F. In a small bowl, combine the crab meat, remaining 2 tablespoons mayonnaise, and Parmesan; stir to blend.

Unroll croissant dough on a work surface in 2 long rectangles; firmly press perforations to seal. Cut each rectangle into 12 squares. Gently press the squares into 2 ungreased 12-cup mini muffin pans, leaving corners of dough extended over edges of cups. Spoon 1 heaping teaspoon crab mixture into each cup. Bake until golden brown, 9–11 minutes. Cool in pan for 2 minutes and transfer to a wire rack to cool to room temperature.

Cut each roast beef slice in quarters for a total of 24 pieces. Cut the quarters into 1-inch squares and arrange evenly on top of crab tartlets. Cut each asparagus spear in thirds and arrange on top of the roast beef (trim to fit if necessary), followed by a dollop of the tarragon sauce. Garnish each with a parsley sprig and serve.

Mini Asian Lettuce Wraps

Makes 24

¹/₂ teaspoon cornstarch

¹/₄ teaspoon garlic powder

¹/₄ teaspoon ground ginger

¹/₄ cup water

2 tablespoons low-sodium soy sauce

2 tablespoons fresh lime juice

1 teaspoon sugar

1 tablespoon olive oil

1 pound boneless, skinless chicken breast, finely chopped

¹/₂ red bell pepper, diced

2 stalks celery, finely diced

2 carrots, peeled and finely diced

2 green onions, thinly sliced

1 head butter lettuce

¹/₄ cup fresh bean sprouts

¹/₄ cup chopped dry-roasted cashews

2 tablespoons chopped fresh mint

In a small bowl, whisk together the cornstarch, garlic powder, and ginger. Add the water, soy sauce, lime juice, and sugar; whisk to blend. Reserve.

Heat oil in a skillet over medium heat. Add chicken and cook until browned, stirring frequently, about 10 minutes. Add the bell pepper, celery, carrots, and green onions; cook until softened, about 5 minutes. Stir in reserved soy sauce mixture. Cook until liquid thickens, 2-3 minutes. (If preparing ahead, cool mixture to room temperature and transfer to a covered container. Refrigerate for up to 24 hours before serving.)

Continued>

Use a sharp knife to cut the core from the lettuce and carefully remove each leaf. Reserve 12 smaller leaves, rinse, and dry on paper towels; use any remaining leaves for a salad or another use. (If preparing ahead, put the dry lettuce leaves in an open plastic bag and refrigerate for up to 24 hours.)

Just before serving, cut each lettuce leaf in half starting at the stem end, removing center vein. Spoon 1 tablespoon of the chicken mixture into each lettuce leaf half and sprinkle with bean sprouts, cashews, and fresh mint. Roll each leaf around the filling in a cylinder and secure with a toothpick. Arrange on a serving platter.

Heavenly Salmon Mousse Bites

Makes 24

1 (8-ounce) package cream
  cheese, softened

2 tablespoons half-and-half

2 tablespoons sour cream

1 (7.5-ounce) can salmon,
  drained, bones and skin
  removed

1 tablespoon minced red
  onion, soaked in cold
  water for 5 minutes and
  drained

Zest of 1 lemon

$1/2$ teaspoon salt

24 Crispy Pastry Cups
  (page 14)

2 tablespoons chopped fresh
  dill, for garnish

In a large bowl, beat the cream cheese, half and half, and sour cream together until smooth. Add the salmon, onion, lemon zest, and salt, beating until blended. Use at once or refrigerate, covered, for up to 4 hours.

Spoon the mousse into the pastry cups and sprinkle with dill.

Coconut Shrimp with Apricot Sauce

Makes about 24

2 eggs

1 cup flaked unsweetened coconut

$^1/_2$ cup panko breadcrumbs

$^1/_2$ cup all-purpose flour

$^1/_2$ teaspoon garlic powder

$^1/_2$ teaspoon paprika

$^1/_4$ teaspoon salt

$^1/_8$ teaspoon freshly ground black pepper

1 pound jumbo shrimp (about 24), peeled, deveined, tails on

Nonstick cooking spray

Apricot Sauce (page xx)

Preheat the oven to 425°F and lightly grease a baking sheet.

In a small bowl, beat the eggs until frothy; reserve. In a second bowl, whisk together the coconut and panko crumbs; reserve. In a third bowl, whisk together the flour, garlic powder, paprika, salt, and pepper; reserve.

Dip the shrimp in the flour mixture, then the egg mixture (letting the excess drip off the shrimp), and then coat in the coconut mixture, pressing to adhere.

Arrange shrimp on the prepared baking sheet in a single layer, about 1 inch apart. Lightly spray with nonstick spray. Bake until the shrimp are golden on the outside and opaque in the center, about 10 minutes.

Serve at once accompanied by Apricot Dipping Sauce, or refrigerate, tightly wrapped, for up to 2 days. Reheat shrimp on a baking sheet in a preheated 350°F oven until heated through, turning once, about 5 minutes.

Apricot Sauce

Makes about 1 cup

2/3 cup apricot jam

2 tablespoons sweet chili
sauce

1 teaspoon apple cider
vinegar

1 teaspoon Dijon mustard

1/4 teaspoon crushed red
pepper flakes

In a small saucepan over medium heat, whisk together
the jam, chili sauce, vinegar, Dijon mustard, and red
pepper flakes; cook until jam melts and mixture is heated
through.

If serving at once, remove from heat and keep warm.
If serving later, cool to room temperature, transfer to
a covered container, and refrigerate for up to 2 days.
Reheat in a small saucepan over medium heat until
mixture bubbles, about 5 minutes.

Dry-Rubbed Riblets

Makes about 12

2 teaspoons paprika

1 teaspoon dried oregano

1 teaspoon sugar

1 teaspoon salt

1 teaspoon ground cumin

$1/2$ teaspoon freshly ground black pepper

$1/8$ teaspoon cayenne pepper

1 small slab baby back ribs (about 2 pounds)

3 tablespoons vegetable oil

Preheat the oven to 300°F and line a baking sheet with heavy-duty aluminum foil.

In a small bowl, combine the paprika, oregano, sugar, salt, cumin, black pepper, and cayenne pepper; whisk until combined.

Use a thin knife to remove the membrane from the bone side of the ribs, and then rub the vegetable oil onto the ribs. Sprinkle the paprika mixture over the ribs and rub evenly into the ribs. Arrange the ribs on the prepared baking sheet.

Bake until tender and juicy on the inside and crispy on the outside, 2–2 $1/2$ hours. Remove from oven, tent with foil, and cool for 20 minutes. Use a sharp knife to cut between each rib and transfer to a serving platter.

Artichoke Cheese Wontons

Makes 24

1/2 cup grated Parmesan cheese

1/2 cup mayonnaise

1/4 teaspoon garlic powder

1 cup grated Monterey Jack cheese

1/2 cup water-packed artichoke hearts, drained and chopped

24 wonton wrappers

Chopped fresh chives, for garnish

In a mixing bowl, combine the Parmesan, mayonnaise, and garlic powder; mix well. Stir in the Monterey Jack and the artichokes. (Mixture can be used at once or refrigerated, covered, for up to 24 hours.)

Preheat the oven to 350°F and spray two 12-cup mini muffin pans with nonstick cooking spray.

Press 1 wonton wrapper into each muffin cup. Bake for 5 minutes, or until edges are lightly browned. (Wrappers can be used at once, or stored in a tightly covered container at room temperature for up to 24 hours; replace in muffin pan before proceeding.)

Fill each cup with 1 rounded tablespoon artichoke mixture. Bake until golden brown, 5–6 minutes. Garnish with chives and serve warm.

Mini Crab Cakes with Mango Chile Salsa

Makes 18

$1/2$ cup panko breadcrumbs, plus extra for sprinkling

3 eggs, lightly beaten

1 teaspoon Dijon mustard

1 teaspoon Worcestershire sauce

$1/2$ teaspoon seafood seasoning (such as Old Bay)

$1/4$ teaspoon salt

1 pound lump crab meat, picked over for shells

$1/2$ cup finely chopped celery

$1/2$ cup cooked fresh, canned, or frozen (thawed) corn kernels, well drained

2 tablespoons minced fresh parsley

2 tablespoons peanut oil

Mango Chile Salsa (page 48)

Sprinkle a baking sheet with panko.

In a medium bowl, whisk together the eggs, mustard, Worcestershire sauce, seafood seasoning, and salt. Add the crab, $1/2$ cup panko, celery, corn, and parsley; stir gently until combined. Form mixture into 18 small patties about $1/2$ inch thick and transfer to the prepared baking sheet. Cover and refrigerate for 1 hour.

In a large, heavy skillet, heat the peanut oil over medium-high until it shimmers. Sauté the crab cakes in batches until golden brown, gently turning once, 2–3 minutes per side. Transfer to paper towels to drain. Arrange on a serving platter and serve warm with Mango Chile Salsa.

Crab cakes can be made ahead and refrigerated, tightly wrapped, for up to 24 hours. Reheat on a baking sheet in a preheated 350°F oven until heated through, 8–10 minutes.

Mango Chile Salsa

Makes about 1 ¼ cups

1 ripe mango, peeled and
finely diced

1 small jalapeño pepper,
seeded and finely diced

¼ cup finely diced red onion

¼ cup finely diced red bell
pepper

1 tablespoon fresh lime juice

3 tablespoons finely chopped
fresh cilantro leaves

Salt and freshly ground black
pepper, to taste

In a small bowl, combine the mango, jalapeño, onion, and bell pepper. Sprinkle with lime juice and stir to combine. Sprinkle with cilantro and mix well. Season with salt and pepper. May be prepared up to 24 hours ahead and refrigerated, tightly covered; pour off any excess liquid and stir before serving.

Fried Artichoke Hearts

Makes about 24

2 eggs

$1/2$ cup milk

$1 1/2$ cups seasoned breadcrumbs

$1/4$ teaspoon garlic salt

$1/8$ teaspoon cayenne pepper

1 (15-ounce) can quartered artichoke hearts, drained and patted dry with paper towels

Peanut oil, for frying

$1/2$ cup butter

1 clove garlic, minced

1 teaspoon fresh lemon juice

$1/4$ cup freshly grated Parmesan cheese

Whisk together the eggs and milk in a bowl and reserve. Place the breadcrumbs, garlic salt, and cayenne pepper in a ziplock bag and shake to combine. Dip artichoke hearts in egg mixture, transfer to bag, and shake to coat with breadcrumbs.

In a large heavy-bottomed pan, pour oil to a depth of 2 inches and heat over medium to 350°F. Fry artichoke hearts, 2 or 3 at a time, until golden brown, about 1 minute on each side. Drain on paper towels. (Fried artichoke hearts can be spread on a parchment-lined baking sheet, covered with plastic wrap, and refrigerated for up to 24 hours. Reheat in a 350°F oven until hot and crispy, 6–8 minutes.)

In a small saucepan, melt the butter and add the garlic. Cook, stirring occasionally, for 3 minutes. Whisk in the lemon juice and cook for 1 more minute. Remove from heat and transfer mixture to a small serving bowl. Arrange warm artichoke hearts on a serving tray and sprinkle with Parmesan cheese. Accompany with toothpicks and the lemon garlic butter for dipping.

Crispy Ham and Gruyère Palmiers

Makes about 36

1 sheet frozen puff pastry,
   thawed and refrigerated

1 heaping tablespoon stone-
   ground mustard

9 slices cooked Black Forest
   ham

1 cup grated Gruyère cheese

Salt and freshly ground
   pepper, to taste

Remove the puff pastry from the refrigerator and unfold on a lightly floured work surface. Use a lightly floured rolling pin to roll dough into a 10 x 12-inch square.

Spread the mustard evenly on the puff pastry. Top with the ham slices and sprinkle evenly with cheese. Sprinkle with salt and pepper. Starting on one long side, roll dough tightly and evenly to the center. Repeat on the other side, so the two rolled sections meet in the middle. Wrap dough tightly in plastic wrap and chill in the freezer for 30 minutes.

Preheat the oven to 400°F and line a baking sheet with parchment paper.

Remove the plastic wrap from the dough and slice with a serrated knife into $1/3$-inch slices. Place each slice on its side on the prepared baking sheet. Bake until crisp and golden, 25–30 minutes. Serve at once or refrigerate, tightly wrapped, for up to 2 days. Reheat on a baking sheet in a preheated 350°F oven until heated through, 5–6 minutes.

Tiny Twice-Baked Potatoes

Makes 36

18 baby red potatoes (about 1 1/4 pounds)

2 tablespoons extra virgin olive oil

Salt and freshly ground black pepper, to taste

1/2 cup grated sharp cheddar cheese

2 tablespoons sour cream

4 slices bacon, cooked and finely crumbled, divided

1 green onion, minced

2 tablespoons butter

1/3 cup heavy cream

Preheat the oven to 400°F and line a baking sheet with parchment paper.

Leaving the skins on, cut potatoes in half lengthwise and transfer to a bowl. Drizzle with olive oil, sprinkle with salt and pepper, and toss until evenly coated. Arrange cut side down on prepared baking sheet. Bake until fork-tender, about 20 minutes. Remove from oven and cool to room temperature.

In a bowl, combine cheese, sour cream, 3/4 of the bacon, and green onion. Using a melon baller or a paring knife and small spoon, carefully scoop flesh from each potato half, leaving a 1/4-inch shell; reserve. Add flesh to cheese mixture. Add butter and cream and mash with a potato masher until well combined. Season with salt and pepper and stir to combine.

Spoon mixture into a heavy-duty ziplock bag and squeeze out excess air. Cut off 1/2 inch of the corner at a diagonal. Pipe mixture into potato cups. Arrange potatoes on a baking sheet and cook at once or refrigerate, covered tightly with plastic wrap, for up to 24 hours.

Preheat the oven to 350°F. Bake potatoes until heated through, 10-15 minutes. Garnish with remaining bacon.

Egg Salad-Stuffed Cherry Tomatoes

Makes 24

12 large red cherry tomatoes

12 large yellow or orange cherry tomatoes (or substitute red)

3 hard-boiled eggs, peeled and finely chopped

$^1/_4$ cup mayonnaise

1 teaspoon yellow mustard

$^1/_4$ teaspoon curry powder

1 tablespoon chopped fresh chives

Salt and freshly ground black pepper, to taste

24 fresh chive stems, halved, for garnish

Cut a $^1/_8$-inch slice off the top of each tomato, and use a grapefruit spoon to remove the inner flesh and seeds. Arrange tomatoes upside down on paper towels to drain. (Tomato shells may be covered with plastic wrap and refrigerated for up to 4 hours before serving.)

Combine the eggs, mayonnaise, mustard, and curry powder in a mixing bowl and mash with the back of a fork until nearly smooth. Add the chopped chives, season with salt and pepper, and stir gently to blend. (Mixture may be prepared up to 4 hours in advance, covered, and refrigerated.)

Fill each tomato shell with egg salad and arrange on a serving platter. Insert 2 pieces of fresh chive vertically in the egg salad of each tomato for garnish.

Parmesan-Spinach Crispies

Makes 24

1 (10-ounce) package frozen chopped spinach, thawed

1/2 cup freshly grated Parmesan cheese

2 green onions, finely chopped

1 tablespoon olive oil

1 tablespoon chopped flat-leaf parsley

1 clove garlic, finely minced

1/4 teaspoon salt

1/8 teaspoon freshly ground black pepper

2 eggs, divided

1 sheet frozen puff pastry, thawed and refrigerated

1 tablespoon water

Preheat the oven to 400°F and lightly grease a 24-cup mini muffin pan.

Press the thawed spinach against a strainer to extract as much liquid as possible. Transfer the drained spinach to a large bowl and add the Parmesan, green onions, olive oil, parsley, garlic, salt, and pepper. Add 1 egg and stir until combined.

Remove the puff pastry from the refrigerator and unfold on a lightly floured work surface. Use a lightly floured rolling pin to roll pastry into a 12-inch square. Cut pastry into 24 squares, and press each square into a muffin cup, draping the corners over the edges. Spoon 1 heaping teaspoon spinach mixture in the center of each pastry square. Fold the corners of the dough over the filling and pinch together in the center.

In a small bowl, beat the remaining egg with the water. Brush the mixture over the tops of the pastries. Bake until puffed and golden, 15–20 minutes. Remove from oven, cool on a wire rack for 2 minutes, and run a sharp knife around the edges of the pan to loosen. Cool to room temperature and remove from pan. Serve at once or refrigerate, tightly wrapped, for up to 2 days. Reheat on a baking sheet in a preheated 350°F oven until heated through, 5–6 minutes.

Crab and Avocado Nachos

Serves 6

1 tablespoon butter

1 jalapeño pepper, ribs removed, seeded, and finely diced

1 cup cooked fresh, canned, or frozen (thawed) corn kernels, well drained

1/2 teaspoon ground cumin

1/2 teaspoon chili powder

1 pound jumbo lump crab meat, picked over for shells

1/2 cup sour cream

Salt and freshly ground black pepper, to taste

Blue and yellow corn tortilla chips

1/2 cup grated Monterey Jack cheese

1 avocado, peeled and cut into 1/4-inch cubes

2 green onions, finely chopped

Preheat an oven broiler on medium heat. Line a baking sheet with aluminum foil and spray with nonstick cooking spray; reserve.

In a small skillet over medium heat, melt the butter and cook the jalapeño until it starts to soften, 2–3 minutes. Add the corn, cumin, and chili powder and cook, stirring occasionally, until mixture bubbles, about 4 minutes. Add the crab meat and sour cream and heat, gently stirring, until mixture is combined and just starts to bubble, 3–4 minutes. Season with salt and pepper.

Arrange a generous layer of chips on the prepared baking sheet and spoon the crab mixture evenly over the top. Sprinkle evenly with the cheese. Broil, watching carefully, until cheese melts, 2–4 minutes. Remove from oven and transfer nachos to a serving platter. Sprinkle with the avocado and green onions.

SKEWERS AND PICKS

Spearing an appetizer on a pick offers the opportunity to creatively layer different complementary flavors. Make a tray of colorful Antipasto Skewers (page 74), for example, and your guests can enjoy the tastes of an entire platter of Italian meats, cheeses, and vegetables in a single handheld bite. Skewering grilled salmon fillet strips makes it easy for your guests to dunk the savory satays in a Thai peanut dipping sauce.

Keep your eyes open for pretty picks, skewers, and cocktail forks in unusual shapes and materials like bamboo, wire, and wood; even lollipop sticks and pretzel sticks can be pressed into service as tiny spears. Canapés on toothpicks couldn't be easier to prepare, and serving is a breeze too. Just set out plenty of napkins and a pretty dish for discarded picks, and no other cutlery is needed.

Toasted Ravioli Pops

Makes about 36

2 tablespoons milk

1 egg

³/₄ cup Italian-style breadcrumbs

¹/₂ teaspoon salt

1 (12-ounce) bag frozen mini cheese- or beef-filled ravioli

Peanut oil, for frying

2 cups prepared marinara sauce

36 lollipop sticks or long cocktail picks

2 tablespoons grated Parmesan cheese

Line a baking sheet with parchment paper. Whisk together the milk and egg in a medium bowl and reserve. Place breadcrumbs and salt in a ziplock bag and shake to combine. Dip the frozen ravioli in the egg mixture, transfer to the bag, and shake to coat with breadcrumbs. Arrange ravioli on prepared baking sheet and put in the freezer for 15 minutes.

In a large heavy-bottomed pan, pour oil to a depth of 2 inches. Heat oil over medium heat until the temperature reaches 350°F. Fry ravioli, a few at a time, until golden brown, about 1 minute on each side. Drain on paper towels. (Ravioli can be spread on a parchment-lined baking sheet, covered with plastic wrap, and refrigerated for up to 24 hours. Reheat in a 350°F oven until hot, 6–8 minutes.)

Heat the marinara sauce in a small saucepan over medium heat until it just starts to simmer. Remove from heat and transfer to a small serving bowl. Insert a lollipop stick or skewer into each ravioli and arrange on a platter; sprinkle with Parmesan cheese. Accompany with marinara sauce for dipping.

Baby Eggplant Parmigiana

Makes about 24

¹/₂ cup all-purpose flour

¹/₄ teaspoon salt, plus extra for sprinkling

¹/₄ teaspoon freshly ground black pepper

2 egg whites

1 cup panko breadcrumbs

¹/₄ teaspoon paprika

2 Japanese eggplants, cut into ¹/₄-inch-thick slices*

²/₃ cup peanut oil

¹/₂ cup grated Parmesan cheese

¹/₂ cup grated mozzarella cheese

1 cup prepared marinara sauce

24 small fresh basil leaves, for garnish

Whisk together the flour, salt, and pepper in a pie plate or shallow bowl. Whisk the egg whites in a bowl until frothy. Whisk the panko and paprika in a separate pie plate or shallow bowl. Dip each eggplant slice in the flour mixture, then in the beaten egg whites, and finally in the breadcrumb mixture to coat completely.

Heat the oil in a heavy-bottom skillet over medium-high heat until it shimmers, 2–3 minutes. Add the eggplant slices in batches and cook until deep golden brown, 1–2 minutes per side; drain on paper towels and sprinkle with salt. (Can be made 1 hour ahead. Let stand at room temperature.)

Continued on page 62.

Preheat the oven broiler and line a rimmed baking sheet with aluminum foil. Arrange the fried eggplant slices 1 inch apart on the baking sheet.

In a small dish, use a fork to combine the Parmesan and mozzarella. Spread 1 heaping teaspoon of the sauce on each eggplant slice. Sprinkle with a rounded teaspoon of the cheese mixture. Broil until cheese melts, about 2 minutes. Remove from oven and cool on pan for 5 minutes. Transfer to a serving platter, top each with a fresh basil leaf, and spear with a small cocktail skewer.

*Long, slender Japanese eggplants are available in specialty markets and larger grocery stores. Unlike regular eggplant, the thin skin of the Japanese eggplant does not need to be peeled. To substitute regular eggplant, cut into $1/4$-inch slices and cut slices into 2-inch rounds with a round cookie or biscuit cutter.

Parma Melon Balls with Citrus-Mint Dressing

Makes 20 to 24

3 tablespoons honey

1/3 cup fresh orange juice

1 tablespoon fresh lime juice

1 large ripe honeydew melon

1 large ripe cantaloupe

1/4 cup fresh mint leaves, thinly sliced

12 (12-inch) bamboo skewers, cut in half

1 pound thinly sliced prosciutto di Parma

Fresh mint sprigs, for garnish

In a small bowl, combine the honey, orange juice, and lime juice and whisk thoroughly. (Dressing can be covered and refrigerated for up to 24 hours.)

Cut the melons in half and remove the seeds. Use a 1 1/2-inch melon baller to scoop as many balls as possible from the honeydew. Use a 1-inch melon baller to scoop as many balls as possible from the cantaloupe. (If you don't have a melon baller, you can cut the honeydew melon into 1 1/2-inch cubes and the cantaloupe into 1-inch cubes.)

Transfer the melon balls to a bowl and drizzle with the honey-citrus dressing. Toss gently to coat then sprinkle with the mint; toss again gently to distribute. Using the pointed end of a skewer, thread 1 honeydew ball and push it down to the blunt end. Follow with 1 cantaloupe ball, pushing it down to just above the honeydew. Fold 1 slice of ham in a frill, and push it over the pointed end of the skewer so it rests atop the cantaloupe ball. Repeat with remaining ingredients and skewers. Arrange skewers standing up with the honeydew end down on a platter. (If necessary, use a sharp knife to cut a thin slice from the bottom of any honeydew melon balls that won't stand up.) Garnish the platter with mint sprigs.

Sesame-Ginger Teriyaki Meatballs

Makes 32 to 36

1 pound lean ground beef

1/2 pound ground pork

1 cup Italian breadcrumbs

1/2 cup milk

1/4 cup chopped fresh parsley

2 eggs, lightly beaten

1 onion, minced

4 cloves garlic, minced, divided

1 teaspoon salt

1/2 teaspoon freshly ground black pepper

1/2 cup soy sauce

1/4 cup plus 1 tablespoon water, divided

2 tablespoons brown sugar

1/4 cup honey

1 (2-inch) piece ginger, peeled and minced

1/2 tablespoon cornstarch

Sesame seeds, for garnish

Finely chopped green onions, for garnish

In a large bowl, combine beef, pork, breadcrumbs, milk, parsley, eggs, onion, half the garlic, salt, and pepper. Beat with an electric mixer for 1 minute. Refrigerate, tightly covered, for 1–8 hours.

Preheat the oven to 350°F and line a baking pan with aluminum foil. Remove beef mixture from refrigerator and shape into 1-inch balls. Arrange 1 inch apart on prepared baking pan. Bake until cooked through and lightly browned, 20–25 minutes. Cool on pan for 5 minutes and transfer to paper towels to drain.

While meatballs bake, combine soy sauce, 1/4 cup water, brown sugar, honey, ginger, and remaining garlic in a saucepan over medium heat; cook, stirring, until sugar is dissolved. In a small bowl, whisk together cornstarch and remaining water. Whisk into sauce and cook just until mixture thickens and starts to bubble. Remove from heat, cover, and keep warm.

Arrange meatballs in a large, shallow dish and drizzle with sauce, stirring to coat. Sprinkle with sesame seeds and green onions; serve with cocktail picks.

Cubano Skewers with Honey Mustard Sauce

Makes 24

1 pound cooked ham, cut into 1-inch cubes

1/2 pound Swiss cheese, cut into 1-inch cubes

1 pound cooked pork loin, cut into 1-inch cubes

24 baby dill pickles

24 (6-inch) skewers

Honey Mustard Sauce (recipe follows)

Layer 1 ham cube, 1 cheese cube, and 1 pork loin cube on a 6-inch skewer, followed by 1 pickle; repeat with remaining ingredients.

Arrange on a serving platter and serve with Honey Mustard Sauce. Skewers may be refrigerated, tightly wrapped, for up to 8 hours before serving.

Honey Mustard Sauce

Makes about 2/3 cup

1/2 cup mayonnaise

2 tablespoons honey

1 tablespoon yellow mustard

Salt and freshly ground black pepper, to taste

In a small bowl, whisk together the mayonnaise, honey, mustard, salt, and pepper. Serve at once or refrigerate, tightly covered, for up to 3 days.

Mini Corn Dogs with Special Sauce

Makes 12

1/2 cup mayonnaise

4 slices dill pickle

2 tablespoons ketchup

1 tablespoon yellow mustard

1/4 teaspoon garlic powder

6 (12-inch) bamboo skewers, cut in half

6 all-beef hot dogs, halved crosswise

1/2 cup all-purpose flour

1/2 cup cornmeal

2 tablespoons sugar

2 teaspoons baking powder

1/4 teaspoon salt

1/4 teaspoon freshly ground black pepper

1/2 to 3/4 cup milk

Peanut oil, for frying

Combine the mayonnaise, pickles, ketchup, mustard, and garlic powder in a food processor and process until smooth. Transfer to a small bowl. (Sauce may be prepared in advance and refrigerated, tightly covered, for up to 2 days.)

Slide each skewer lengthwise through 1 hot dog half, leaving at least a 1 1/2-inch handle.

In a bowl, whisk together the flour, cornmeal, sugar, baking powder, salt, and pepper. Add 1/2 cup milk and whisk until combined, adding more milk if necessary until the consistency of thick pancake batter. Transfer batter to a large, tall glass for easier dipping.

In a large heavy-bottomed saucepan, pour the peanut oil to a depth of 4 inches and heat over medium to 350°F. One at a time, dip each skewered hot dog in the batter until completely covered, tilting the glass if necessary. Carefully slide the hot dogs into the hot oil. Fry 1 or 2 at a time until golden brown, 2-3 minutes. Drain on paper towels. Repeat with remaining hot dogs and batter.

Serve warm accompanied with the sauce for dipping.

Bacon-Wrapped Chévre-Stuffed Apricots

Makes 16

16 slices bacon (about 1 pound)

16 large (whole) dried apricots, such as Turkish apricots

¼ pound goat cheese, softened

⅓ cup maple syrup

¼ teaspoon freshly ground black pepper

Preheat the oven to 400°F and line a baking sheet with parchment paper.

Arrange the bacon on prepared baking sheet and bake until the fat is released and the bacon just starts to brown but is still flexible, about 15 minutes. Remove from oven and drain on paper towels. (When baking sheet is cool, discard paper and re-line with a new sheet of parchment paper.)

Use a sharp knife to open a hole in one side of the apricot, and then spread some of the goat cheese inside. Repeat with remaining apricots and cheese. Wrap 1 strip of bacon around each apricot and skewer with a toothpick. Arrange on prepared baking sheet. (Use at once, or cover pan with plastic wrap and refrigerate for up to 4 hours. Let pan sit out at room temperature for 30 minutes before proceeding.)

In a small bowl, whisk together the maple syrup and pepper; reserve. Brush the bacon-wrapped apricots with the maple syrup mixture. Bake for 10 minutes.

Remove from oven, turn apricots over, brush with more maple syrup glaze, and continue baking until bacon is crispy, about 10 more minutes. Arrange on a platter and serve warm.

Prosciutto-Wrapped Pears with Watercress and Brie

Makes 16

1 tablespoon fresh lemon
   juice

1 tablespoon water

2 ripe Bartlett or Bosc pears

6 ounces thinly sliced
   prosciutto ham, halved
   lengthwise

1 cup fresh watercress leaves
   (or substitute arugula)

4 ounces Brie cheese, cut
   into 16 small wedges

In a large bowl, combine the lemon juice and water. Cut the pears in half, remove cores, and cut each half in 4 slices. Add the pear slices to the lemon juice mixture and toss to coat the cut sides.

Lay 1 slice of prosciutto on a work surface. Top with 1 pear slice (blot any excess moisture with a paper towel), 1 sprig of watercress, and 1 wedge of Brie. Roll up and secure with a toothpick. Repeat with remaining ingredients and arrange on a serving tray. Serve at once or refrigerate, tightly wrapped, for up to 2 hours before serving.

Roast Beef, Gorgonzola, and Balsamic-Roasted Grape Skewers

Makes about 24

2 tablespoons balsamic vinegar

1 1/2 tablespoons minced shallot

1 tablespoon olive oil

1 teaspoon dark brown sugar

1/4 teaspoon salt

48 seedless red grapes (about 2 cups)

1 pound deli-sliced rare roast beef

1 (4-ounce) wedge Gorgonzola cheese

Freshly ground black pepper

Preheat the oven to 425°F. In a bowl, combine the balsamic vinegar, shallot, olive oil, brown sugar, and salt. Add the grapes and toss to coat.

Transfer grapes to a 9 x 13-inch baking pan and roast, uncovered, for 20 minutes, stirring once halfway through cooking. Remove from oven and cool in pan to room temperature. (Grapes can be prepared in advance and refrigerated, tightly covered, for up to 8 hours. Bring to room temperature before proceeding.)

Cut the roast beef into 24 pieces. Cut the Gorgonzola into 24 cubes. Thread onto the skewer 1 folded slice of roast beef, 1 grape, 1 piece of Gorgonzola, and another grape. Arrange on a serving platter and sprinkle with pepper.

Cheesy Sausage Nibbles

Makes about 48

1 1/4 cups all-purpose flour

1 1/2 teaspoons baking powder

1/2 teaspoon salt

1/4 teaspoon freshly ground black pepper

1/4 teaspoon cayenne pepper

2 cups grated cheddar cheese

1 pound bulk pork sausage

1 small Vidalia onion, finely chopped

3 tablespoons butter, melted

Preheat the oven to 400°F and line a baking sheet with parchment paper.

In a large bowl, whisk together the flour, baking powder, salt, black pepper, and cayenne pepper. Add the cheese and use two forks to toss until cheese is coated with flour mixture. Add sausage, onion, and butter and use hands to thoroughly combine mixture. Roll into 1-inch balls and arrange 1/2 inch apart on prepared baking sheet.

Bake until balls are golden and cooked through, about 25 minutes. (May be prepared ahead and refrigerated, tightly covered with plastic wrap, for up to 24 hours. Reheat in a 400°F oven until hot, 5-6 minutes.) Spear with toothpicks and serve warm.

Antipasto Skewers

Makes 24

12 (12-inch) skewers, cut in half

24 pitted black olives

24 small pepperoncini peppers

24 small fresh mozzarella balls

12 jarred quartered and marinated artichoke hearts, halved

24 slices salami, folded in quarters

24 pimiento-stuffed green olives

1 large red bell pepper, seeded and cut into 24 pieces

Thread ingredients onto skewers in this order: black olive, pepperoncini, mozzarella ball, artichoke heart, salami, green olive, and bell pepper. Serve immediately or refrigerate, tightly covered, for up to 1 day.

Deconstructed Bacon Jalapeño Poppers

Makes 24 pieces

8 slices thick-cut bacon

2 cups grated sharp cheddar cheese

4 ounces cream cheese, softened

12 small or 6 large jalapeño peppers

Cut each slice of bacon into 3 pieces. Transfer bacon to a large skillet and cook over medium heat, stirring frequently, until brown and crispy. Remove from heat and use a slotted spoon to spread the bacon flat on paper towels to drain; reserve.

Preheat the broiler. Line a baking sheet with aluminum foil.

Combine cheddar and cream cheese in a small bowl and mix well. Remove the stems from the jalapeños, cut in half lengthwise, and remove the seeds. (If using large jalapeños, cut each piece in half again horizontally for a total of 24 pieces.) Spread cheese mixture evenly in the jalapeño halves. Arrange on the prepared baking sheet and broil until mixture melts and bubbles, 3-4 minutes. Remove from oven and cool on a wire rack for 5 minutes.

Top each stuffed jalapeño with a piece of the bacon and secure with a toothpick. Transfer to a platter and serve. Poppers may be refrigerated, tightly wrapped, for up to 24 hours. Reheat on a baking sheet in a 350°F oven until heated through, turning once, about 5 minutes.

Mini Cheese Balls

Makes 36

8 ounces cream cheese, softened

1/2 cup grated cheddar cheese

2 tablespoons salted butter, softened

2 teaspoons fresh lemon juice

1/8 teaspoon Worcestershire sauce

1/8 teaspoon hot sauce

1/8 teaspoon freshly ground black pepper

1 cup coating (choose one or several):

Finely crumbled crisply cooked bacon

Finely chopped chives or flat-leaf parsley

Finely chopped pistachios or toasted pecans

Lightly toasted white or black sesame seeds

Finely snipped dried cherries or cranberries

36 pretzel sticks

Line a baking sheet with parchment paper. In a bowl, combine the cream cheese, cheddar cheese, butter, lemon juice, Worcestershire sauce, hot sauce, and pepper. Stir until well combined and smooth.

Measure out 2 teaspoons of the mixture and use hands to shape into a ball. Shape the remaining mixture into approximately 35 similarly sized balls. Roll the balls in coatings of your choice and arrange on the prepared baking sheet. Cover tightly with plastic wrap and chill for 24 hours, or freeze for up to 2 weeks (defrost overnight in refrigerator before serving). Before serving, insert a pretzel stick in the center of each ball and arrange on a platter.

Honey Sriracha–Glazed Bacon-Wrapped Scallops

Makes 15 to 20

2 tablespoons honey

2 teaspoons Sriracha sauce

2 teaspoons olive oil

1 pound (15-20) fresh or frozen (thawed) sea scallops, patted dry

$1/2$ pound thinly sliced bacon, halved crosswise

To make the glaze, whisk together the honey, Sriracha, and olive oil in a small bowl; reserve. (Glaze may be used at once or refrigerated, covered, for up to 3 days.)

Wrap each scallop with a half slice of bacon and secure with a toothpick. (Bacon-wrapped scallops may be cooked at once or covered and refrigerated for up to 6 hours.)

Preheat the oven broiler and line a baking sheet with aluminum foil. Arrange the scallops on the prepared baking sheet. Brush both sides with glaze mixture. Broil, turning once, until scallops are opaque and bacon is crispy, 3-4 minutes per side.

Greek Salad on a Stick

Makes 16

1 small sweet red onion, cut into 16 (¹/₂-inch) pieces

32 small ripe grape tomatoes

16 pitted Kalamata olives, well drained

¹/₂ pound feta cheese, cut into 16 small cubes

1 thin English cucumber, cut into ¹/₂-inch slices

¹/₂ head iceberg lettuce, cut into 16 (1 x 1-inch) wedges

8 (12-inch) bamboo skewers, cut in half

2 tablespoons extra virgin olive oil

Salt and freshly ground black pepper, to taste

2 teaspoons chopped fresh oregano, or ¹/₂ teaspoon dried oregano, for garnish

Before preparing the skewers, soak the onion slices in cold water for 5 minutes. Drain.

Thread 1 onion slice, 1 tomato, 1 olive, 1 feta cube, 1 cucumber slice, 1 lettuce wedge, and another tomato onto a skewer. Repeat with remaining skewers. Drizzle with the olive oil and sprinkle with salt and pepper. Garnish with oregano and serve.

Salmon Satay with Thai Peanut Dipping Sauce

Makes 8 to 12

1 ½ pounds salmon fillets, skin and bones removed

6 (12-inch) bamboo skewers, cut in half and soaked in water for 30 minutes to prevent burning

½ teaspoon lemon pepper

½ teaspoon garlic powder

½ teaspoon salt

⅓ cup soy sauce

⅓ cup firmly packed dark brown sugar

⅓ cup water

¼ cup peanut oil

Thai Peanut Dipping Sauce (recipe follows)

Cut the salmon fillets in strips about 1 inch by 4 inches. Twist bamboo skewer lengthwise into each piece of fish. Sprinkle evenly on both sides with lemon pepper, garlic powder, and salt.

In a small bowl, stir together the soy sauce, brown sugar, water, and peanut oil until sugar is dissolved. Place salmon skewers in a large ziplock bag with the soy sauce mixture, seal, and turn to coat. Refrigerate for at least 2 hours and up to 8 hours.

Preheat the grill to medium heat, about 350°F. Lightly oil the grill grate. Place salmon skewers on the preheated grill, discarding marinade. Cook, turning over once, until salmon has light grill marks and is opaque on the outside but still slightly undercooked in the center, about 1 ½ minutes per side. Transfer to a serving platter and accompany with Thai Peanut Dipping Sauce.

Thai Peanut Dipping Sauce

Makes 1 ⅓ cups

1 cup canned light coconut milk

⅓ cup natural creamy peanut butter

2 teaspoons dark brown sugar

1 tablespoon soy sauce

1 teaspoon Sriracha sauce

Heat the coconut milk in a small saucepan over medium heat just until it begins to boil. Reduce heat and whisk in the peanut butter, brown sugar, soy sauce, and Sriracha. Simmer, whisking occasionally, until mixture thickens slightly, about 5 minutes. Remove from heat and keep warm. Sauce can be cooled, covered, and refrigerated for up to 1 day. Reheat sauce before serving.

Candied Bacon and Pineapple Spears

Makes 24

1 1/2 cups firmly packed brown sugar

2 tablespoons Sriracha sauce

1/4 teaspoon freshly ground black pepper

12 thin strips bacon, halved crosswise

1 fresh pineapple, peeled and cut into 24 spears (3 inches long x 1/2 inch thick)

12 (12-inch) bamboo skewers, cut in half and soaked in water for 30 minutes to prevent burning

Heat a barbecue grill to medium heat and lightly oil the grate.

In a pie plate or shallow dish, combine the brown sugar, Sriracha, and pepper. Dredge the bacon in the mixture, coating both sides. Thread each pineapple spear lengthwise on a skewer. Wrap evenly with the bacon, securing ends with toothpicks. Cook at once, or arrange on a pan, cover with plastic wrap, and refrigerate for up to 8 hours.

Lay bacon-wrapped pineapple spears on the grate and grill, watching carefully and turning often, until bacon is crispy, 5-7 minutes. Cool for 5 minutes before transferring to a serving platter.

Macadamia-Crusted Chicken Bites with Honey Mustard Dipping Sauce

Makes 24

1/2 cup mayonnaise

2 tablespoons honey

1 tablespoon yellow mustard

1 egg

2 tablespoons milk

1/8 teaspoon salt

1/8 teaspoon freshly ground black pepper

1 cup finely chopped roasted macadamia nuts

1 1/2 pounds boneless, skinless chicken breasts, cut into 24 chunks

In a small bowl, combine the mayonnaise, honey, and mustard; stir until well blended. Sauce may be used at once or refrigerated, tightly covered, for up to 3 days.

Preheat the oven to 400°F and line a baking sheet with aluminum foil.

In a shallow dish, combine the egg, milk, salt, and pepper. Pour the macadamia nuts in a separate shallow dish. Dip the chicken pieces in the egg mixture followed by the chopped nuts, rolling to coat. Arrange chicken pieces on prepared baking sheet.

Bake, turning once, until chicken is cooked through and golden brown, 18-20 minutes. Cool on pan for 5 minutes then arrange on a serving platter. Insert a cocktail pick into each chicken piece and serve accompanied with honey mustard sauce.

SLIDERS AND MINI SANDWICHES

Whether you create a sandwich on toast, a mini roll, or a soft little bun, sliders and mini sandwiches offer an endless variety of breads and fillings.

While eating a full-sized meatball sub requires a big appetite, you can enjoy the same savory flavors in a bite or two with saucy Italian Meatball Sliders (page 118). Or treat your guests to a taste of New England with Baby Lobster Rolls (page 92). Mini Grilled Cheese Sandwiches (page 114) capture the melty goodness of the classic childhood favorite with a sophisticated twist—a dipping sauce made from slow-roasted tomatoes.

From open-faced crostini to mini cheeseburgers, pint-sized sandwiches are perfect for hearty appetites and game-day gatherings.

Tarragon Chicken Salad Puffs

Makes 36

8 ounces boneless, skinless chicken breast

$1/4$ teaspoon celery seed

$1/4$ teaspoon salt

1 green onion, finely minced

1 hard-boiled egg, peeled and finely chopped

$1/4$ cup mayonnaise

$1/4$ teaspoon fresh lemon juice

$1/4$ teaspoon minced fresh tarragon leaves

$1/4$ cup finely chopped celery

Salt and freshly ground black pepper, to taste

36 Tiny Choux Puffs (page 19)

Place the chicken breasts in a large saucepan and add enough cold water to cover. Add the celery seed and salt and bring the water to a boil over high heat. Reduce the heat to medium and poach for 15 minutes, or until the chicken loses its pink color. Remove from heat and let chicken cool in the poaching liquid for 15 minutes. Remove chicken from the broth with a slotted spoon and finish cooling it in the refrigerator, covered, for 3-4 hours. Chop the chicken finely and reserve.

Combine the onion, egg, mayonnaise, and lemon juice in a bowl. Add the tarragon, celery, reserved chicken, salt and pepper, and stir. Use at once or chill in the refrigerator, tightly covered, for up to 24 hours.

To assemble the appetizers, spoon a generous teaspoon of filling into the bottom half of each choux puff. Replace the tops and press gently before arranging on a serving platter.

Photo on page 18.

Baby Lobster Rolls

Makes 24

24 small soft dinner rolls

1/2 cup salted butter, melted

1 cup mayonnaise

2 tablespoons fresh lemon juice

2 tablespoons chopped fresh dill

1 tablespoon chopped fresh chives

1/2 teaspoon lemon zest

1/4 teaspoon seafood seasoning (such as Old Bay)

2 pounds cooked lobster, finely chopped

1/3 cup finely chopped celery

Salt and freshly ground black pepper, to taste

Chopped fresh flat-leaf parsley, for garnish

Fresh Dill Sprigs, for garnish

Preheat the oven to 350°F.

Use a serrated knife to cut down the center of each roll without cutting all the way through. Arrange the rolls on a baking sheet. Gently open the rolls and brush with melted butter. Bake until lightly browned, 5-6 minutes. Remove from oven and cool on a wire rack to room temperature. Rolls may be prepared ahead and stored at room temperature, tightly wrapped, for up to 1 day.

In a bowl, combine the mayonnaise, lemon juice, dill, chives, lemon zest, and seafood seasoning. Add the lobster and celery and stir gently to combine. Season with salt and pepper. Mixture may be prepared ahead and refrigerated, tightly covered, for up to 1 day.

Fill each roll with 1 rounded tablespoon of the lobster mixture and garnish with parsley and dill.

French Dip Sliders with Au Jus

Makes 24

24 Baby Sesame Slider Rolls
(page 12)

4 tablespoons salted butter,
melted

1 pound thinly sliced roast
beef, quartered

¹/₂ pound sliced provolone
cheese, quartered

Au Jus (page 96)

Preheat the oven to 350°F and lightly grease a 9 x 13-inch baking dish.

Split rolls in half and arrange bottom halves in the prepared baking dish; brush lightly with melted butter. Top with roast beef and provolone and cover with tops of sliced rolls. Brush with remaining butter. Cover with foil and bake until hot and cheese is melted, about 15 minutes. Rolls can also be covered and refrigerated for up to 24 hours before baking. (If reheating, increase baking time to 20–25 minutes.)

Pour Au Jus in 24 shot glasses or small cups. Serve each slider on a small plate accompanied by a cup of Au Jus.

Au Jus

Makes about 2 ¹/₂ cups

1 tablespoon butter

1 shallot, chopped

2 cloves garlic, minced

2 ¹/₂ cups beef stock or broth

1 tablespoon Worcestershire
   sauce

Salt and freshly ground black
   pepper, to taste

In a saucepan, melt the butter over medium heat. Add the shallot and garlic and cook until softened, 3-4 minutes. Add beef stock, Worcestershire sauce, and salt and pepper; bring to a boil. Lower heat and simmer for 10 minutes.

Remove from heat and use at once, or refrigerate, tightly covered, for up to 2 days. Return to saucepan and bring to a boil over medium heat before serving.

Pita Bites

Makes 16

8 ounces cream cheese, softened

1/2 cup mayonnaise

2 green onions, minced

1/2 teaspoon dried dill

1/4 teaspoon garlic salt

1/4 teaspoon freshly ground black pepper

4 whole pitas, split horizontally

4 large leaves butter lettuce

1 pound deli-shaved smoked honey ham

1/2 pound thinly sliced Havarti cheese

16 frilly sandwich toothpicks

Combine the cream cheese, mayonnaise, onions, dill, garlic salt, and pepper. (Mixture can be prepared in advance and refrigerated, tightly covered, for up to 2 days. Bring to room temperature before proceeding.) Spread the mixture on the inside surfaces of the pitas.

On 4 pita halves, evenly layer the lettuce leaves, ham, and cheese. Top with remaining pita halves. (May be refrigerated, tightly covered, for up to 8 hours.) Cut each pita into 4 wedges and secure each wedge with a frilly toothpick.

Beef, Asiago, and Caramelized Onion Sliders

Makes 24

2 tablespoons butter

2 Vidalia onions, halved and cut into 1/4-inch slices

Salt and freshly ground black pepper, to taste

24 Baby Sesame Slider Rolls (page 12), split

1 1/2 cups grated Asiago cheese

1 pound thinly sliced deli roast beef

12 dill pickle sandwich slices, halved crosswise

Melt the butter in a large skillet over medium-low heat. Add the onions and cook, stirring occasionally, until they turn a deep golden brown, 40-45 minutes. Season with salt and pepper, remove from the pan, and let cool.

Heat the oven to 350°F and line 2 baking sheets with aluminum foil. Arrange the roll tops cut side up on one baking sheet and roll bottoms cut side up on the other; bake until lightly toasted, about 4 minutes. Remove from oven, sprinkle with cheese, and return to oven. Bake just until cheese melts, 2-3 minutes.

Remove from oven and divide the roast beef among the bottom rolls. Top each slider with caramelized onions, 1 halved pickle slice, and a top roll. Arrange on a platter and serve.

Kobe Beef Sliders with Secret Sauce

Makes 24

6 tablespoons butter, softened, divided

4 tablespoons minced onion

Salt and freshly ground black pepper, to taste

2 pounds ground Kobe beef or sirloin

6 slices American cheese, quartered

24 Baby Sesame Slider Rolls (page 12), split and toasted

24 round dill pickle slices

24 small lettuce leaves

3 Roma tomatoes, each thinly sliced crosswise into 8 slices

Secret Sauce (recipe follows)

Melt 4 tablespoons butter in a small pan. Add onions and cook until softened, 2–3 minutes. Season with salt and pepper; reserve. (If preparing ahead, mixture may be refrigerated, tightly covered, for up to 2 days. Reheat in a saucepan over medium heat for 2–3 minutes.)

Divide the ground beef into 18 portions and shape into small patties, about $1/2$ inch thick; season with salt and pepper. Melt the remaining 2 tablespoons butter in a large skillet over medium heat. Cook the burgers in batches, turning once, until cooked through and lightly browned on each side, 4–5 minutes, topping with cheese during the final 30 seconds of cooking. Transfer to paper towels to drain. (If preparing ahead, burgers can be refrigerated, tightly covered, for up to 1 day. Reheat on a baking sheet in a 350°F oven until hot, about 10 minutes.)

Spread the onion mixture on the bottom half of the rolls. Top each with a burger, pickle slice, lettuce leaf, and tomato slice. Spread the top half of each roll with Secret Sauce and place on top, pressing gently. Arrange sliders on a platter and serve.

Photo on page 13.

Secret Sauce

Makes about 1 cup

- 1/2 cup mayonnaise
- 1/4 cup ketchup
- 1/4 cup finely chopped dill pickles
- 1 teaspoon yellow mustard
- 1/2 teaspoon garlic powder
- 1/4 teaspoon paprika

In a small bowl, combine all ingredients and stir until well blended. Use at once or cover and store in refrigerator for up to 3 days.

Open-Faced Reubens

Makes about 20

1 (1-pound) loaf thinly sliced cocktail rye bread

1 cup Thousand Island Dressing (recipe follows)

1 1/2 pounds thinly sliced corned beef, quartered

1 1/2 cups sauerkraut, well drained

3/4 pound thinly sliced Swiss cheese, quartered

Preheat the oven broiler on high and line a baking sheet with aluminum foil.

Arrange bread slices in a single layer on prepared baking sheet. Spread each slice with 2 teaspoons Thousand Island Dressing. Top with corned beef followed by sauerkraut and Swiss cheese, dividing evenly among bread slices. Broil, watching carefully, until cheese melts and edges start to brown, 3–5 minutes. Serve warm.

Thousand Island Dressing

Makes about 1 1/2 cups

1 cup mayonnaise

1/4 cup cocktail sauce

1 hard-boiled egg, finely chopped

2 tablespoons ketchup

1 tablespoon minced onion

2 teaspoons dill pickle relish

1 clove garlic, minced

1/4 teaspoon salt

1/8 teaspoon freshly ground black pepper

In a small bowl, combine all ingredients and stir gently to blend. Use immediately, or cover tightly and refrigerate for up to 2 days.

Mini Chicken and Cheese Quesadillas

Makes 25

1 1/2 cups grated cheddar cheese

4 ounces cream cheese, softened

1 1/4 cups finely chopped cooked chicken

1 large Anaheim pepper, seeded and finely chopped

1/4 teaspoon freshly ground black pepper

10 (10-inch) flour tortillas

3 tablespoons butter, melted

Salt, for sprinkling

2 ripe avocados, peeled and cubed

1/4 cup prepared salsa

Salt and freshly ground pepper to taste

In a medium bowl, combine the cheddar and cream cheese and stir to blend. Add the chicken, Anaheim pepper, and black pepper; stir until combined. Mixture may be used at once or refrigerated in a tightly covered container for up to 1 day. (If refrigerated, let sit at room temperature for 1 hour before continuing.)

Preheat the oven to 375°F and line a baking sheet with aluminum foil.

Using a round 2-inch biscuit cutter, cut 5 rounds from each tortilla (50 rounds total). Brush half of the tortilla rounds with melted butter, and arrange them butter side down on prepared baking sheet. Top each with a heaping tablespoon of the chicken mixture. Top with the remaining tortilla rounds, brush with butter, and sprinkle with salt. Bake until quesadillas are lightly browned, about 15 minutes, turning over once halfway through cooking time.

Meanwhile, mash the avocados with the salsa in a small bowl and stir to blend; season with salt and pepper. Remove quesadillas from oven and cool on pan for 5 minutes before transferring to a serving platter. Serve accompanied by guacamole.

Avocado Toasts with Balsamic Glaze and Cherry Tomatoes

Makes 24

24 Golden Crostini (page 15)

2 large ripe avocados, peeled and each cut into 12 slices

Balsamic Glaze (recipe follows)

Salt and freshly ground black pepper

1 cup mixed yellow and red cherry tomatoes, halved, drained on paper towels

Chopped fresh flat-leaf parsley, for garnish

Top each crostini with 1 avocado slice and use a knife to smash and spread evenly to the edges. Season with salt and pepper. Drizzle lightly with the Balsamic Glaze (you may have extra). Divide the tomatoes among the crostini and garnish with parsley. Arrange on a platter and serve at once.

Balsamic Glaze

Makes about 1 cup

1 cup balsamic vinegar

1/4 cup firmly packed light brown sugar

Combine balsamic vinegar with brown sugar in a heavy-bottomed saucepan over medium heat. Cook, stirring constantly, until sugar has dissolved. Bring to a boil, reduce heat to low, and simmer until mixture is reduced by half, about 20 minutes. Let cool to room temperature. Glaze may be stored in a covered glass container in the refrigerator for up to 3 weeks. For easy drizzling, pour the glaze into a squeeze bottle with a fine tip.

Creamy Mushroom and Caramelized Onion Crostini

Makes 24

3 tablespoons butter, divided

3 tablespoons olive oil, divided

2 yellow onions, halved and thinly sliced

1/4 cup white wine or chicken broth

1 1/2 pounds mushrooms of your choice, sliced 1/4 inch thick

1/3 cup heavy cream

Salt and freshly ground black pepper, to taste

24 Golden Crostini (page 15)

2 tablespoons minced fresh chives

Melt 1 tablespoon of butter in a large, heavy skillet over medium-high heat. Add 1 tablespoon olive oil and stir to combine. Add onions and cook, stirring occasionally, until translucent, about 5 minutes. Reduce heat to medium and add the wine. Continue cooking, stirring often, until onions are a deep brown color and caramelized, 20-30 minutes. Reserve. (Mixture can be transferred to a tightly covered container and refrigerated for up to 2 days. Reheat in a saucepan over medium heat before proceeding.)

Melt remaining 2 tablespoons butter in a large, heavy skillet over medium-high heat. Add remaining 2 tablespoons olive oil and stir. Add mushrooms and cook, stirring occasionally, until they release their liquid and are golden brown, 15-20 minutes. Increase heat to high, add cream, and cook, stirring constantly, until mixture comes to a low boil. Remove from heat and season with salt and pepper.

Arrange crostini on a serving platter and spoon caramelized onions onto each piece. Top with the mushroom mixture and garnish with chives. Serve warm.

Asparagus Rolls

Makes 24

24 fresh asparagus spears

8 ounces cream cheese, softened

3 ounces mild blue cheese, crumbled

2 tablespoons mayonnaise

1 tablespoon chopped fresh chives

1/4 teaspoon freshly ground black pepper

12 bread slices, crusts trimmed

12 thin slices smoked ham

4 tablespoons butter, melted

Paprika, for sprinkling

Cut each asparagus spear to a length of 6 inches (discard ends) and arrange in a steamer basket over boiling water. Cover and steam just until crisp-tender, 4-6 minutes. Drain in a colander and rinse with cool water to stop cooking. Drain on paper towels. (Asparagus spears may be covered with plastic wrap and refrigerated for up to 1 day.)

In a small bowl, combine the cream cheese, blue cheese, mayonnaise, chives, and pepper. (Mixture may be prepared ahead and refrigerated, tightly covered, for up to 1 day.)

Preheat the oven to 400°F and lightly grease a baking sheet.

Flatten each bread slice with a rolling pin. Spread 1 side of each slice with 2 tablespoons cream cheese mixture and top with 1 ham slice. Lay 2 asparagus spears facing opposite directions at one end of each bread slice; roll up and place seam side down on prepared baking sheet. Brush with melted butter and sprinkle with paprika. Bake until golden brown, about 12 minutes. Cool for 5 minutes and use a sharp knife to cut in half. Transfer to a serving platter and serve warm.

Mini Tuna Melts

Makes 24

2 tablespoons minced red
  onion

2 (6-ounce) cans oil-packed
  Albacore tuna, drained

1/2 cup mayonnaise

1 1/2 teaspoons whole-grain
  mustard

2 stalks celery, finely
  chopped

1 teaspoon minced fresh
  flat-leaf parsley

Salt and freshly ground black
  pepper, to taste

24 Golden Crostini (page 15)

1 1/2 cups grated sharp
  cheddar cheese

Preheat the broiler on high and set the rack about 4–5 inches from the heat source. Line a large baking sheet with aluminum foil. Soak onion in cold water for 5 minutes. Drain.

In a bowl, break up the tuna with a fork. Add the mayonnaise, mustard, celery, onion, and parsley; stir to combine. Season with salt and pepper and stir to combine. Mixture can be used at once or refrigerated, tightly covered, for up to 6 hours. (If refrigerated, let bowl sit out at room temperature for 1 hour before using.)

Arrange crostini on prepared baking sheet, spread with the tuna mixture, and sprinkle with cheese. Cook under the broiler until the cheese melts, watching carefully, 3–5 minutes. Arrange on a platter and serve immediately.

Mini Muffuletta Sandwiches

Makes 24

1 cup pimiento-stuffed green olives, chopped

1/4 cup pitted black olives, chopped

1/4 cup sliced pepperoncini, chopped

2 cloves garlic, minced

2 tablespoons drained capers

1 stalk celery, chopped

1 tablespoon finely chopped red onion

1/2 teaspoon dried oregano

1/2 teaspoon dried basil

1/2 teaspoon freshly ground black pepper

1/2 teaspoon celery seed

1/3 cup Italian dressing

24 Baby Sesame Slider Rolls (page 12), split

12 thin slices Swiss cheese, quartered

12 thin slices deli ham, quartered

12 thin slices provolone cheese, quartered

12 slices Genoa salami

In a large bowl, combine the green olives, black olives, pepperoncini, garlic, capers, celery, onion, oregano, basil, pepper, and celery seed. Stir until well combined. Drizzle with the Italian dressing and stir until well combined. Mixture may be used at once or refrigerated in a tightly covered container for up to 1 week.

Preheat the oven to 350°F and line a baking pan with aluminum foil.

Spread 1 heaping tablespoon of the olive salad evenly over each cut side of roll bottoms. Top each with 2 pieces Swiss, 2 pieces ham, 2 pieces provolone, 2 pieces salami, and 1 generous tablespoon of the olive mixture. Cover with roll tops and arrange sandwiches on prepared baking pan. Cover with another piece of foil and seal edges around pan. Bake until cheeses melt and sandwiches are hot, 14–16 minutes.

Mini Grilled Cheese Sandwiches with Roasted Tomato Dipping Sauce

Makes 24

12 slices white bread

2 tablespoons butter, softened

6 (¹/₄-inch-thick) slices Colby cheese

Roasted Tomato Dipping Sauce (recipe follows)

Heat a large griddle or skillet over medium heat. Spread one side of the bread slices with the butter.

Place 1 bread slice butter side down and top with 1 slice of cheese. Top with another piece of bread, butter side up. Cook until lightly browned and flip over. Continue cooking until both sides are golden and cheese is melted. Repeat with the remaining bread and cheese.

Allow the sandwiches to cool slightly. Use a sharp knife to trim off the crusts and cut each sandwich into 4 thin rectangles. Arrange on a serving platter and serve warm accompanied by the tomato sauce for dipping.

Roasted Tomato Dipping Sauce

Makes about 3 cups

1 pound Roma tomatoes

1 onion, quartered

6 cloves garlic, unpeeled

3 tablespoons olive oil

1 teaspoon salt

$1/2$ teaspoon freshly ground black pepper

1 to 2 tablespoons water

Preheat the oven to 250°F.

Cut the tomatoes in half lengthwise and gently remove the seeds. Place the tomatoes, onion, and garlic cloves on a baking sheet; drizzle with the olive oil and sprinkle with salt and pepper, tossing well to coat. Turn the tomatoes cut side down and cook for 2 hours, stirring occasionally.

Remove from oven, reserve garlic, and transfer the tomatoes, onion, and pan juices to a food processor or blender. Add 1 tablespoon of the water and pulse to blend. Squeeze the cooked garlic into the mixture and purée until smooth, adding additional 1 tablespoon water if necessary. Serve warm. (Sauce may be prepared in advance and refrigerated, tightly covered, for up to 2 days.) Reheat in a small saucepan over medium heat before serving.

Shrimp Remoulade Pita Crisps

Makes 36

3/4 cup mayonnaise

2 tablespoons whole-grain
  mustard

1/4 cup finely chopped green
  onions

2 teaspoons fresh lemon juice

1 clove garlic, minced

1/2 teaspoon salt

1/4 teaspoon freshly ground
  black pepper

1/4 teaspoon paprika

1 celery root* (about 1 pound)

2 tablespoons finely chopped
  dill pickle

1 pound peeled, deveined
  baby shrimp, cooked

36 Garlic Pita Crisps (page 11)

2 tablespoons chopped fresh
  flat-leaf parsley

In a large bowl, whisk together the mayonnaise, mustard, green onions, lemon juice, garlic, salt, pepper, and paprika.

Working quickly to prevent browning, peel the celery root and chop finely; transfer immediately to mayonnaise mixture and stir until well coated. Add pickle and shrimp and stir gently to combine. Use at once or refrigerate, covered, for up to 4 hours.

Arrange the pita crisps on a serving platter and spoon the shrimp mixture on top; garnish with parsley.

*Celery root, also known as celery knob or celeriac, is available in specialty markets and larger grocery stores. If not available, chopped celery may be substituted; for best results, use pale-green inner stalks.

Italian Meatball Sliders

Makes 24

1 pound bulk Italian sausage

1 pound ground beef chuck

1/2 cup Italian-style breadcrumbs

1/3 cup milk

2 cloves garlic, minced

1/2 teaspoon salt

Freshly ground black pepper to taste

2 tablespoons olive oil, divided

2 cups prepared marinara sauce

24 dinner rolls, split and toasted

2 cups grated mozzarella cheese

Thoroughly combine the sausage, beef, breadcrumbs, milk, garlic, salt, and pepper in a large bowl. Roll into 24 balls, each about 1 1/2 inches.

Heat 1 tablespoon of the olive oil in a large nonstick skillet over medium heat. Add half of the meatballs and cook, turning, until browned all over, about 5 minutes. Drain on paper towels and repeat with remaining 1 tablespoon olive oil and meatballs. Drain the oil, wipe the skillet with a paper towel, and pour in the marinara sauce. Add the meatballs, cover, and simmer over medium heat for 20 minutes. (Mixture can be cooled and refrigerated, tightly covered, for up to 24 hours. Reheat in a saucepan over medium heat until sauce bubbles and meatballs are heated through before proceeding.)

Arrange the dinner roll bottoms on a serving platter and sprinkle with half the cheese. Top each with a meatball and some of the sauce. Sprinkle with the remaining cheese and replace the tops of the rolls. Serve warm.

Mini Pulled Pork Barbeque Stacks

Makes 24

1 Boston butt pork roast (about 3 pounds)

1 tablespoon garlic powder

1 tablespoon paprika

1 1/2 teaspoons dark brown sugar

1 1/2 teaspoons celery salt

1 1/2 teaspoons mustard powder

1 teaspoon salt, plus extra for seasoning

1/2 teaspoon cayenne pepper

1 1/2 cups water

Freshly ground black pepper to taste

24 Baby Sesame Slider Rolls (page 12), split and toasted

1 cup prepared barbeque sauce

1 cup prepared coleslaw

Preheat the oven to 225°F. Use a sharp knife to cut a crosshatch pattern in the outer fat of the pork roast approximately 3/4 inch deep and 1 inch wide. In a small bowl, whisk together the garlic powder, paprika, brown sugar, celery salt, mustard powder, 1 teaspoon salt, and cayenne pepper until well blended. Rub the mixture all over the pork roast. Place the pork in a roasting pan and pour the water into the pan. Cover with aluminum foil and roast for 3 hours, checking occasionally and adding more water if necessary.

Remove the foil and continue roasting until the pork has reached an internal temperature of 190°F, about 1 1/2 hours longer. Remove from oven, cover roast loosely with foil, and let rest for 30 minutes. Remove fat and shred the pork using 2 forks. Toss the meat with the pan juices and season with salt and pepper. (Pork may be transferred to a tightly covered container and refrigerated for up to 48 hours. Warm in a saucepan over medium heat until hot and bubbling before proceeding.)

Arrange roll bottoms on a large platter and top with a heaping tablespoon of pork. Drizzle with barbeque sauce and top with a spoonful of coleslaw. Gently press upper rolls on top.

Prosciutto, Pear, Fig, and Brie Toasts

Makes 16

1 loaf French bread

4 tablespoons butter, softened

1 cup fig jam

16 thin slices prosciutto (about ¼ pound)

2 pears, each cut into 16 thin slices

1 pound Brie cheese, thinly sliced

Salt and freshly ground black pepper, to taste

Preheat the oven to 450°F and line a baking sheet with aluminum foil.

Cut 16 (½-inch-thick) slices from the loaf of bread. Butter both sides of each slice and arrange on prepared baking sheet. Spread 1 tablespoon of fig jam on each bread slice. Top with 1 slice of prosciutto and 2 slices of pear. Top with the Brie slices then season with salt and pepper. Bake until the cheese is melted, 8–10 minutes.

Index

Metric Conversion Chart

VOLUME MEASUREMENTS		WEIGHT MEASUREMENTS		TEMPERATURE CONVERSION	
U.S.	METRIC	U.S.	METRIC	FAHRENHEIT	CELSIUS
1 teaspoon	5 ml	1/2 ounce	15 g	250	120
1 tablespoon	15 ml	1 ounce	30 g	300	150
1/4 cup	60 ml	3 ounces	80 g	325	160
1/3 cup	80 ml	4 ounces	115 g	350	175
1/2 cup	125 ml	8 ounces	225 g	375	190
2/3 cup	160 ml	12 ounces	340 g	400	200
3/4 cup	180 ml	1 pound	450 g	425	220
1 cup	250 ml	2 1/4 pounds	1 kg	450	230

About the Author

Eliza Cross is the award-winning author of a dozen cookbooks, including the acclaimed *Pumpkin It Up!* and the perennially popular *101 Things To Do With Bacon*. A food stylist, corporate recipe developer, and marketing consultant, she blogs about cooking, gardening, and home DIY projects at Happy Simple Living. Eliza lives with her family in Denver.